All It Takes Is A Conversation

By Jerry Ferszt

"To speak and be heard with love is the highest art of being human."

Published by Sacred Keystone Press. 2026

Printed in the United States of America
First Edition

ISBN: 979-8-218-90766-2

For information, contact:
jferszt92@gmail.com

Dedication

For Nicole—
my muse, my partner, my mirror.
Thank you for always being willing to have the conversation,
even when it's hard, even when it's messy,
especially when it matters.
This book exists because of the space we've created together.

Table of Contents

Author's Note

I didn't set out to write a book with answers.

This started as a collection of observations—things I noticed in my own life, in my relationships, and in the quiet moments when conversations lingered longer than expected. Over time, those observations began to form a pattern. Again and again, the moments that led to real change weren't dramatic events or big realizations. They were conversations. Sometimes spoken. Sometimes internal. Sometimes avoided for far too long.

I began to see how much of our discomfort comes not from what we feel, but from what we never quite say. How often we sense something is off but don't have the language—or the courage—to bring it into the open. How easily silence can masquerade as peace, and how much energy it takes to keep certain truths buried.
This book isn't a guide to communication in the traditional sense. It isn't about techniques, scripts, or winning difficult conversations. It's about something more basic and more human: what happens when we slow down enough to notice what's already present, and allow ourselves to speak from that place instead of around it.

Everything in these pages comes from lived experience. From conversations that went well and conversations that didn't. From moments of clarity and moments of avoidance. From learning, often the hard way, that honesty doesn't require aggression, and that listening—real listening—is one of the most underestimated forms of care we have.

My hope is not that you agree with everything here, but that something in it helps you listen differently. To yourself. To the people you care about. To the subtle signals that tell you when a conversation is needed, even if it feels inconvenient or uncomfortable.

This book is meant to be read slowly. There's no rush to get through it, and no pressure to apply it perfectly. If it does anything at all, I hope it creates a little more space—space to pause, to reflect, and to speak more honestly when it matters.
That's where all meaningful change I've witnessed has begun.

Introduction – All It Takes Is A Conversation

There's a phrase that has quietly guided me through some of the most important moments of my life:

"All it takes is a conversation."

It sounds simple. And in a way, it is. But don't mistake simplicity for smallness. That phrase is a key. A doorway. An entire worldview. It's the reminder that everything we seek—clarity, healing, opportunity, intimacy, peace—begins with the willingness to speak.

I've started businesses, repaired relationships, sidestepped disaster, and built dreams—all because I was willing to have the conversation. The one that felt awkward. The one that could've been ignored. The one that held the key to everything shifting.

We often think magic is something outside of us—something rare, mysterious, or hard to access. But I've come to believe that magic lives in language. That the ability to take a thought, a feeling, a hope, a truth—and give it form through words—is one of the most sacred powers we have. It's how we plant seeds in other people's hearts. It's how we unlock the hidden doors in our own.

This book is about that magic.

It's about the conversations we have with ourselves, with our loved ones, with the people who challenge us, and with the world around us. It's about reclaiming the courage to speak—and the grace to listen. It's about healing what was silenced. Expanding what's possible. And remembering that your voice doesn't just describe your life—it *creates* it.

You don't need to be a great speaker. You don't need to always know what to say. You just need to be willing to *begin*.

Because sometimes, all it takes to change everything...
is a conversation.

Part I – Conversations With Self

Chapter 1: The Mirror Inside

There is a moment most of us avoid.

It doesn't arrive loudly. There's no announcement when it shows up. It usually comes in quiet—early in the morning, late at night, or in the brief pause between one obligation and the next. It's the moment when there's nothing left to respond to, no one needing us, no task demanding attention.

It's the moment we're alone with ourselves.

That's often when we reach for something. A phone. A distraction. A plan. A story about what we'll do next. Anything that pulls our attention outward before it has a chance to turn inward.

Not because we're weak.
Not because we're broken.
But because we already sense what might be waiting there.

The mirror.

Not the physical one hanging in a bathroom or hallway—but the internal one. The place where we see ourselves without filters, explanations, or defenses. The place where the stories we tell ourselves begin to thin out. Where the version of who we *say* we are and who we *actually* are stand side by side.

The mirror doesn't accuse.
It doesn't raise its voice.
It doesn't demand change.

It simply reflects.

And that's what makes it uncomfortable.

Most of us are taught—explicitly or implicitly—to stay outward-facing. Be productive. Be useful. Be improving. If something feels off, fix it. If something hurts, distract yourself. If something doesn't make sense, move faster.

Even self-improvement can become a way to avoid the mirror. As long as we're working on the next version of ourselves, we don't have to sit with the current one. As long as we're gathering tools, advice, and frameworks, we can stay busy instead of honest.

We're rarely taught how to pause without judgment.
How to look without flinching.
How to sit with a truth without immediately trying to turn it into an action plan.

So when the mirror appears, we often look away—not consciously, but instinctively. We fill the space. We rationalize. We explain. We tell ourselves we'll come back to it later.

Later rarely comes.

Because the mirror asks something simple, but not easy:
Are you willing to see what's already here?

Not what you wish were true.
Not who you're becoming.
Not who you've convinced others you are.

Just what is.

For a long time, I didn't realize how skilled I had become at avoiding that moment. I was reflective enough to sound self-aware, but not still enough to be truly honest. I could talk about growth, values, and intention—but there were patterns I hadn't fully named, truths I hadn't let settle.

Not because I didn't know them.
But because knowing something intellectually is very different from letting it land.

The mirror doesn't force that landing. It waits.

It waits while we build lives, relationships, and identities around stories that feel safer than the truth. It waits while we blame circumstances, systems, or other people for tensions we haven't examined internally. It waits while we perfect explanations that sound reasonable enough to keep us moving forward.

And eventually—if we slow down long enough—it reflects something we can't unsee.

Maybe it's a contradiction.
Maybe it's a resentment we've been justifying.
Maybe it's a role we've outgrown but continue to perform.

Maybe it's a truth we've been circling for years without naming.

The mirror doesn't tell us what to do with what we see.

That part is up to us.

This is where many people misunderstand self-honesty. They assume it's about harshness, self-criticism, or tearing themselves apart. But the mirror isn't cruel. If anything, it's neutral. It doesn't shame. It doesn't comfort. It doesn't soften the edges—but it doesn't sharpen them either.

It simply shows.

What we bring into that moment determines what happens next.

Some people glance and leave.
Some negotiate.
Some argue internally.
Some make promises they don't intend to keep.

And some stay.

Staying doesn't mean solving everything. It doesn't mean immediate change. It doesn't even mean clarity. Often, it just means allowing a truth to exist without trying to manage it.

That alone can be unsettling.

Because once a truth is acknowledged—even quietly—it begins to influence how we move through the world. It shows up in our conversations. Our reactions. Our silences. The way we listen. The way we deflect.

This is why the first conversation that matters isn't with another person.

It's with yourself.

How you speak internally becomes the template for how you speak externally. If you rush past your own discomfort, you'll rush others. If you defend against your own truths, you'll struggle to hear someone else's. If you can't sit with what's unresolved inside you, you'll feel the urge to fix, correct, or control conversations that don't need fixing.

The mirror sets the tone.

Not by giving instructions—but by revealing where you're already standing.

This book isn't about forcing that moment. No one can do that for you. And honestly, they shouldn't try. Transformation doesn't happen because someone else insists—it happens when you're ready to stay a little longer than you usually do.

To look a little more closely.
To listen a little more carefully.
To stop rushing toward the next answer.

Before we talk about relationships, conflict, healing, or change—this is the ground we stand on. Not perfection. Not certainty. Just honesty.

And even that doesn't have to be complete.

It only has to be real.

Because every meaningful conversation that follows—every one that heals, clarifies, or connects—will quietly trace back to this moment.

The moment you chose not to look away.

Chapter 2: Choosing Responsibility Over Victimhood

The moment you stop outsourcing your power, everything changes.

There's a moment—quiet, often invisible to the outside world—when something shifts inside you. You stop asking, *"Why is this happening to me?"* and start asking, *"What is this trying to show me?"* That moment is the bridge between victimhood and responsibility. It doesn't look dramatic, but it is revolutionary.

Victimhood isn't just a reaction to pain—it can become a *home*. A well-decorated place of safety, identity, and even belonging. When you've been hurt, misunderstood, dismissed, or betrayed, it's easy to make your pain into your story. And then, without realizing it, your story becomes your personality. Your personality becomes your defense. And your defense becomes the reason you can't change.

The tricky part is, most of this happens subconsciously. No one walks around thinking, *"I've chosen to identify with my suffering."* It happens quietly. Slowly. Over time. And usually with good reason.

You may have learned that attention only comes when you're hurting.

You may have learned that safety only exists in silence.
You may have learned that if you don't protect your pain, no one else will.

But what starts as survival often becomes stagnation.
And the longer you live in that space, the more any invitation to take responsibility feels like an attack.

Because when pain becomes your identity, healing can feel like death.

Responsibility ≠ Blame

This is where many people get stuck, so it's worth slowing down.

Taking responsibility does not mean blaming yourself.
It does not mean denying what happened.
And it does not mean excusing the behavior of others.

Responsibility is about ownership—not fault.

It's the moment you realize that while you may not have chosen what happened, you *do* get to choose what happens next. You get to decide how much authority the past has over your present.

Responsibility sounds like:

- *This happened. It hurt. And now I choose how I respond.*

- I can feel the pain without becoming the pain.

- I can honor what happened without giving it authority over what happens next.

This isn't about gaslighting yourself into pretending things were okay. It's about realizing that carrying the wound forever doesn't protect you.
It imprisons you.

The Role of Conversation

Victimhood often survives in silence.
Or in echo chambers that reinforce the same story.
It thrives on avoidance, justification, or blame loops.
What it cannot survive is truth.

And the thing is... *truth rarely lives in isolation.*
It comes out through **conversation**.

When you sit with someone who sees you without enabling you—who listens without feeding your fear—something powerful happens. You start to hear yourself differently. You start to ask better questions. You stop defending your pain and start dissolving it.

Sometimes, that conversation is with a friend.

11

Sometimes, it's with a therapist.
Sometimes, it's with a journal.
Sometimes, it's with the younger version of you who still thinks being hurt means being broken.

But wherever it happens, something shifts when you stop circling the pain and start *relating* to it differently.

You don't dissolve the wound by ignoring it.
You dissolve it by bringing it into the open without turning it into your identity.

The Choice That Changes Everything

There is power in saying:

-I'm not waiting for an apology to heal.

-I don't need the world to change for me to be free.

-I am not what happened to me—I am what I choose next.

Choosing responsibility isn't always loud. Often, it's barely noticeable from the outside. It might look like responding differently than you used to. Not engaging the same argument. Not telling the same story for the hundredth time.

But internally, it's seismic.

Every small shift in response creates a crack in the old pattern.
And enough cracks let the light in.

Story: "The Blame Game Ends Here"

Andre had been carrying resentment like it was oxygen.
Against his ex. Against his parents. Against the job that never saw his worth.
He wouldn't have called himself a victim—he just believed he was right.
And everyone else was wrong.

He was the one who had given more than he got.
The one who was loyal, and always left behind.
The one who tried—and kept losing.

So when his therapist asked him, *"What's the common denominator in all these stories?"* he felt his chest tighten.

He wanted to say, *"Bad luck. Cruel people. Unfair systems."*
But what he said was, *"Me."*

He hated the word as soon as it left his mouth.
It felt like betrayal. Like self-blame. Like letting them off the hook.

But then the therapist asked another question.

"What if that's not blame? What if that's where your power lives?"

That question haunted him for days.

Until one morning, instead of re-reading the angry text thread with his ex like he had so many times before, Andre deleted it.

Not to forget.
But to stop keeping score.

He didn't send a final message.
He didn't post a cryptic quote.
He just let go.

And something inside him cracked—not in a breaking way, but in a softening way.
Like a muscle unclenching.
Like a pressure releasing.
Like a door unlocking.

That was the moment he stopped needing to be right, and started needing to be free.

He didn't forgive everything that had happened right away.
But he started living like he didn't need it to happen again.

And from that day forward, his story wasn't about what they did. It was about what he chose to do next.

Chapter 3: Listening to Your Higher Self

Excitement is not a feeling—it's a compass.

There's a version of you that already knows.
Not just about what to do next, but about who you are, why you're here, and what you're capable of becoming.
It's not the voice of fear or logic.
It's not the voice of the past or the crowd.
It's quiet—but unshakable.
It speaks in symbols, in nudges, in feelings. It's the voice of your **higher self.**

Most people are so tuned into the noise of the world that they miss the wisdom inside. They confuse their thoughts with truth. They think if it's loud, it must be important.

But your higher self doesn't yell. It whispers. And it usually speaks through excitement, alignment, peace, or resistance. It speaks through the feeling you get when you're about to say yes to something that lights you up—or no to something that drains your soul.

To hear it, you have to slow down. You have to create space between the stimulus and the response. You have to ask yourself not just what's *safe*, but what's *true*. And that's not easy, because it means trusting something deeper than logic. It means admitting that your deepest clarity might not make sense to anyone else—and choosing it anyway.

Excitement is one of the most misunderstood signals in human experience. People think it's a fleeting emotion. But it's not. **It's a compass**. It's the energetic signature of something meant for you. When something excites you in a way that expands your chest or lights up your mind—it's often your higher self saying, *"Yes. This."*

But listening requires courage. Because when you hear that "yes," you're often called to step outside the comfort zone. You're asked to release the familiar and walk into the unknown. That's the real initiation—not into something mystical, but into something *authentic*.

Listening to your higher self doesn't mean you'll never feel fear again. It means your *faith becomes louder than your fear*. It means you trust that there's a deeper order to life, and that when you follow your truth, the path rises to meet you.

This is the third conversation.
The one where you tune into your soul—not as a concept, but as a guide.
And when you begin to walk in alignment with that voice, you stop seeking permission.
You start moving as though you've already been chosen—because in a way, you have.
Chosen by your own knowing.
And nothing is more powerful than a human aligned with their truth.

But what exactly is your *higher self*? And how do you know when it's speaking?

Your higher self is the clearest, most untainted version of you—the you beneath your conditioning, beyond your fears, beyond your pain. It's the part of you that isn't trying to prove anything or protect anything. It's rooted in trust. When you tune into it, you don't feel manic or desperate. You feel calm. You feel ready.

One of the biggest traps is mistaking the ego for the guide. The ego is reactive. It's loud. It's obsessed with being right, being liked, or being safe. But your higher self doesn't need to be right. It just needs to be real. When you learn to pause before reacting—when you breathe and drop into stillness—you start to distinguish between fear and truth. Between noise and knowing.

Your higher self will often ask more of you than you thought you were capable of. It may nudge you to say no when people expect a yes. It may push you to create, to leave, to begin, or to rest—at times that seem irrational to others. That's why it takes practice to trust it. Because the deeper your alignment, the more it may require you to stand alone.

But here's the paradox: when you follow that voice, you don't lose yourself—you find yourself. When you stop chasing approval and start chasing truth, you become whole again. That wholeness radiates. It magnetizes. It heals.

You don't have to "find your purpose" by chasing a path. You find it by listening inward. Your soul already knows.
The real work is unlearning all the noise that made you doubt it.

Story: "The Leap"

Maya had everything going for her—on paper.
A stable job in the city. A well-furnished apartment. A partner who, by all appearances, was loyal and kind. She had spent years building this life, and even longer convincing herself it was the one she wanted.

But something didn't sit right. Not in any dramatic way—just a quiet ache.
Every morning, she woke up and stared at the ceiling just a little too long.
Every night, she told herself, *"This is fine. This is what adulthood looks like."*

Then one morning, standing in her kitchen with a cup of coffee, she heard it.
Not out loud, but inside.

"You're not supposed to be here."

It wasn't angry.
It wasn't urgent.
It just felt… true.

She tried to brush it off. She told herself she was being ungrateful. That people had it worse. That her job paid well and her relationship was stable.

But the voice didn't go away. It kept tugging. Not with panic—but with a strange kind of peace.

One day, she walked past a community garden tucked between two buildings. She didn't know why she stopped. She didn't garden. She didn't have time. But something about the smell of soil and laughter and sunlit stillness cracked something open inside her.

That night, she stayed up researching permaculture and small-scale farming.
Two weeks later, she applied to volunteer.
Three months after that, she broke her lease, ended her relationship, and moved to a small plot of land upstate that offered live-in work for growers.

Her friends called her brave.
Her family called her crazy.
But for the first time in her life, *she called herself whole.*

Maya never looked back—not because it was easy, but because for the first time in years, she felt alive. Every dirt-stained hand, every aching muscle, every conversation under starlight with new friends felt like medicine.

She didn't have a five-year plan.
But she had something better—peace.
And she knew that wherever her higher self led next, she'd listen.

Part II – Conversations With Others

Chapter 4: Speaking Truth to Power

If Part I was about reclaiming your voice within, Part II is about using that voice to reshape the world around you. Because once you've remembered who you are, the next step is to show up in truth—to speak from that place, even when it's uncomfortable, even when the stakes are high.

Speaking truth to power doesn't always look dramatic. It isn't always a public stand or a bold confrontation. Sometimes it means telling a friend they hurt you. Telling your boss that something isn't working. Telling your partner what you really want. Speaking truth to power can look like saying no, like setting a boundary, like asking a question no one else will ask. It doesn't always shake the room. Sometimes it just shifts the energy—and that's enough.

Most people don't avoid truth because they're dishonest. They avoid it because they're afraid. Afraid of being rejected, misunderstood, punished, or seen as "too much." We're conditioned to play small, to avoid conflict, to seek harmony even at the cost of honesty. But that kind of harmony is hollow. It's not real peace—it's a truce between people who are too scared to be known.

But here's the thing: **when you silence yourself to make others comfortable, you abandon the part of you that was meant to lead.**

Truth-telling is not about being right. It's about being real. It's not about overpowering someone—it's about refusing to abandon yourself. You don't speak your truth because you know how it will be received. You speak it because it's yours. Because your voice, when aligned with your inner compass, is a force of clarity. And clarity is contagious.

The truth doesn't just free you—it frees everyone around you. It signals safety. It invites transparency. It sets the tone for what's possible in a relationship, in a workplace, in a movement. It creates a ripple effect where others begin to feel, *"If they can speak up... maybe I can too."*

It's worth saying again: **truth is not the enemy of peace—it is the beginning of peace.** That peace might not be instant. It might shake things up first. Peace built on silence is fragile. It depends on avoidance. Peace built on truth has roots. It can handle tension without collapsing.

Speaking truth to power doesn't mean you'll always be received well. Sometimes things *do* shake before they settle. Sometimes relationships change. Sometimes systems resist.

But when you stay grounded in what's real for you, you stop needing approval to stand where you stand.

And that's where power actually lives.

Not in domination.
Not in control.
But in alignment.

Power isn't only something you confront.
It's something you claim.

Story: "The Night They Finally Talked"

James and his father had been walking around each other for years —polite, distant, cordial. Their conversations rarely broke the surface: weather, sports, work. Anything deeper brought visible discomfort.

Growing up, James had longed for emotional connection. But his father was a product of a generation that believed strength meant silence. That emotions were best handled privately—or not at all. James learned early that tears were awkward, vulnerability was weakness, and love was something you showed, but rarely said.

When James became a father himself, something cracked. He

wanted to raise his son differently. He wanted to teach him how to speak his truth. But every time he tried, he felt that old lump in his throat—the fear that he didn't know how. Because he'd never seen it modeled.

One Thanksgiving night, after everyone else had gone to bed, James found himself sitting with his father by the fire. The air was thick with unsaid things.

After a long silence, James said it.

"I don't really know how to talk to you. And I wish I did."

His father didn't speak right away. He stared into the flames like they might offer him a script. Then he said, with a voice rougher than usual, *"Me neither."*

More silence. But not the avoidant kind. The honest kind.
Then James said, *"I think I learned how to hold back from watching you."*

His father exhaled hard.
"Yeah. I think I learned that from mine."

No tears. No big dramatic reconciliation. Just two men sitting with the truth.
That was the conversation that changed everything.

It didn't fix their entire history. But it cracked the shell. It created space for something new.

In the months that followed, they talked more. Not constantly—but more honestly. James started asking his father questions about his childhood. His father started showing up to James's son's baseball games, not just to spectate—but to connect.

All because of one night, one conversation, and the willingness to be the first one to go first.

Chapter 5: The Space Between Us
(The Importance of Open Dialogue in Relationships)

"The distance between two people isn't always measured in feet or miles. Sometimes, it's measured in unspoken truths."

The space between two people in any relationship is a living thing. It breathes. It tightens. It softens. It fills with tension or ease, depending on what is said—or not said. Every conversation adds something to that space. It either builds a bridge or deepens the divide.

Sometimes, what needs to be said is obvious. But more often, the real transformation happens when someone takes the risk to express something difficult, vulnerable, or unpolished—and the other person listens without rushing to correct, defend, or judge.

That kind of listening is rare. And sacred.

We often think of powerful communication as articulate speaking —finding the right words, expressing the right thought, landing the perfect phrase. But the most transformative conversations don't start with speaking. They start with **listening**.

And not just waiting for your turn to talk. Not listening to reply. But listening to **understand**.

Truly listening requires humility. You have to accept that the other person's inner world is just as rich and nuanced as yours, even if they haven't yet found the words to express it. You have to be willing to hear past the frustration, past the tone, past the flinching defenses—and listen for what's underneath.

This type of listening is **generous**. You're offering your presence without judgment. You're holding space for the other person to come to their own realizations, in their own time.

It's also a radical act of healing.

When someone feels **truly heard**, they soften. When they soften, they can reflect. When they reflect, they can speak more clearly. And that's when truth begins to move between people, not just inside of them.

Words are just one part of the story. There's also **tone**—what's behind the words. There's **body language**—how someone shifts, where their eyes go, how their shoulders hold. There's **what's not said**—the silences that stretch, the topics avoided, the sighs between sentences.

Listening means becoming present to all of this. It means paying attention not only to the words, but to the feelings behind the words.

Some people never learned how to express their truth. They grew up in homes where vulnerability was punished or ignored. They learned that saying how they felt would be used against them—or simply wouldn't matter.

So when you're in relationship with someone like that—romantic, family, friend—you become a kind of sacred ground. A space where expression can grow again.

That doesn't mean you fix them. It means you **hold space**.

You don't demand perfection. You offer patience. You don't rush clarity. You invite unfolding. You understand that for many, just finding their voice is the work of a lifetime.

When someone is allowed to express poorly—awkwardly, messily, imperfectly—without being shut down, they get better. Just like any skill, **expression grows with safety and time**.

So often, people say things they don't quite mean—not because they're careless, but because they're still learning how to be honest. They're still learning to identify their own truth in the moment. It's messy work. But when you stay present in those moments, you allow the space between you to become a place of transformation, not trauma.

Story: "I Just Needed a Minute"

They sat in silence for the third time that week, each on opposite ends of the couch, both pretending to scroll through their phones. It wasn't a loud silence—it was the kind that hums with everything unsaid.

Earlier, she had tried to explain something that had been bothering her, and it hadn't come out right. Her tone had been sharp. His face had tensed. Neither of them had meant to shut the other down, but somehow, they ended up here again—quiet, distant, unresolved.

Finally, he set his phone down. *"I'm not mad,"* he said. *"I just… I didn't know what you needed from me."*

She blinked. No one had ever asked her that before—not like that. In her childhood, when things got hard, people got louder. Or they disappeared. You figured things out on your own.

"I don't know," she said honestly. *"I'm not used to explaining what I need."*

He nodded. *"Okay. Then let's figure it out together."*

She looked at him, surprised not just by the words, but by how gently he said them. No expectation. No pressure. Just presence.

30

That moment didn't solve everything. But it changed the space between them. Because for the first time, she realized she didn't have to come into the conversation already knowing everything. She just had to show up. And he just had to *listen*.

Sometimes, love sounds like *"Let's figure it out together."*
And sometimes, that's the conversation that changes everything.

Story: "The Thing He Was Afraid to Say"

Eli wasn't the type to talk about feelings. He fixed things. Quietly. With his hands. With long drives and small gestures. When things felt off with Mia, he didn't bring it up. He just made dinner. Or changed the oil in her car. Or held her a little longer at night.

But lately, something had been building in him. A pressure he couldn't release through doing. He felt distant from her. Not because she had done anything wrong—but because he couldn't find the words to say what was wrong in *him*.

One night, while they sat on the porch watching the sun go down, she asked gently, *"Are you okay?"*

He almost said *"I'm fine,"* like he always did. But instead, something cracked.

"I don't know how to tell you when I'm not okay," he said, his voice barely above a whisper. *"I've never been good at this. I'm afraid if I say the wrong thing, I'll mess it up. That you'll think less of me."*

She didn't interrupt. She didn't rush in to fix it. She just nodded, eyes soft, and said, *"Then just say anything. We'll figure it out from there."*

That moment didn't turn Eli into a master communicator overnight. But it gave him permission to be a beginner. It gave him the safety to try.

And sometimes, that's all we really need.

Story: "The Table at the Market"

It was a cool Saturday morning, and June was sitting in her car with the engine running, watching vendors unfold tables and pop-up tents across the gravel lot. Her heart pounded. Her hands were cold, even though she'd been gripping the steering wheel for twenty minutes. Her tote bags full of neatly labeled herbal salves and teas sat quietly in the back seat—packed, prepared, and possibly destined to go right back home.

She'd almost turned around twice already. The voice in her head was screaming louder than ever.

You don't belong here. Who's going to buy anything from you? You're not a real herbalist. You're just someone who plays with plants. These people are professionals. This isn't you.

June had thought the fear would go away once she arrived. It didn't. It sat in her chest like a stone. But behind that fear, there was another feeling—quieter, but steady: *You've come this far. Just have the conversation.*

She turned the car off, stepped out, and carried her boxes over to the folding table she'd reserved at the very edge of the market. It wasn't in the busy center near the produce vendors or the local coffee truck—it was tucked by the tree line. Forgotten. Hidden. *Perfect*, she thought.

By the time she arranged her jars and handwritten signs, her palms had stopped sweating. But her voice still caught in her throat every time someone walked by.

Until he showed up.

A man in a weathered denim jacket, carrying a mug of coffee, stopped in front of her table and picked up a jar of comfrey salve.

"You make this?"

She hesitated. *"Yeah. I grow everything myself. It's all wildcrafted. No fillers. Just what the plants want to do."*

33

He nodded slowly, reading the label. Then he picked up another jar. *"This is good. It smells real. Clean."*

June waited for the polite nod and walk-away. Instead, he asked questions. Real ones. He asked about where she sourced her ingredients, how she learned to make her blends, and whether she'd ever worked with groups. She told him—awkward at first, then with more ease—the truth: she'd never sold anything before today. She'd studied plants her whole life. She just hadn't spoken much about it. Until now.

"I run a retreat center outside town," he said finally, setting the jar down with care. *"We bring people in for healing. Workshops, retreats, quiet time. I've been looking for someone who can teach a more earth-based approach. You ever thought about that?"*

Her mouth opened, but no words came out at first. She almost said no. Almost apologized. Almost backed out of her own dream.

But something stronger rose up from inside her—the part that had brought her here in the first place.

"Yes," she said. *"Yes, I have."*

They exchanged numbers. A month later, June was standing in a circle of twelve people at the edge of a meadow, holding fresh yarrow in one hand and a bundle of cedar in the other. She spoke without notes. Her voice was calm. Clear. Rooted.

She had always belonged here. She just hadn't said it out loud yet.

All it took... was the conversation.

The Thread That Connects It All

Each of these stories carries a different energy—hesitation, repair, vulnerability, breakthrough. But the common thread is simple: *someone chose to speak when silence would have been easier.*

These are not grand speeches. They're not perfectly timed monologues. *They are ordinary words spoken with presence.* And that's the magic of conversation—it turns the ordinary into the sacred. It builds bridges over silence. It breaks patterns that have lasted generations. It brings opportunities to life that would've passed by unnoticed.

Whether it's a partner learning to express themselves, a person learning to listen, or a dream waiting to be claimed, the moment a conversation begins, *so does transformation.*
Because in the space between two people, or between who you've been and who you're becoming—**a single conversation can change everything.**

Chapter 6: Conflict as Creative Tension

Most people treat conflict like a fire: dangerous, destructive, something to be put out as quickly as possible. But what if we saw it differently?

What if conflict wasn't a sign that something is broken...
...but that something is ready to *change*?

At its core, conflict is just **energy with direction but no resolution yet**. It's the space where values collide, where needs surface, where identities are challenged and growth is on the table —but only if we can stay present long enough to move through it, instead of away from it.

We've been taught that conflict is bad. That disagreement means disrespect. That if tension arises, the relationship is unstable. But the truth is, most of the strongest, most aligned relationships you'll ever see have walked through fire together—not because they avoided conflict, but because they learned to **use it**.

Healthy conflict is not a fight—it's a **conversation with friction**. And friction isn't failure. Friction polishes. It sharpens ideas. It brings clarity. It burns away illusion. When approached with curiosity instead of defensiveness, conflict becomes *creative tension*

—a dynamic space where something new can emerge.

But this shift only happens when both people understand the deeper truth: the relationship is not the conflict. The conflict is just what's *visiting* the relationship.

To navigate conflict consciously, you must learn to:

Pause before reacting.

Listen beneath the words for the real need being expressed.

Speak from "I" rather than accuse with "you."

Stay in the room—not just physically, but emotionally.

Trust that truth can deepen love, not destroy it.

And most importantly, you must stay curious. Ask questions like:

"What's this really about for you?"

"What are you needing that you're not getting?"

"What are you protecting right now?"

These questions break the loop. They turn conflict from a closed system of reactivity into an open field of possibility. They remind both people that this tension doesn't have to push them apart—it can pull them deeper.

Because when two people can stay present with each other in the heat of disagreement, they build a relationship that isn't just resilient—it's alive.

And just like every chapter before this one, it starts with the willingness to speak.
To listen.
To stay.

Because conflict doesn't destroy connection.
Avoidance does.

Chapter 6.5: When Truth Feels Like a Threat

Holding Space Without Losing Yourself

Not everyone will welcome your truth.

That's one of the hardest lessons in learning to speak honestly—
and one of the most freeing. You can speak gently. You can speak
clearly. You can speak with love, patience, and care. And still,
someone may shut down, lash out, get offended, or feel threatened.

That doesn't mean you spoke poorly.
It means something real was touched.

Truth has a way of disrupting what's been held together by
avoidance. Not violently. Not maliciously. But unmistakably. It
brings into focus what's been tolerated, buried, or protected for a
long time.

And when someone has built their identity around survival, denial,
or comfort, your truth can feel like a threat—not to who they are,
but to the *story* they've used to keep themselves safe.

That doesn't make them bad.
That makes them human.

But it also doesn't make their reaction your responsibility to fix.

Mediation ≠ Martyrdom

Yes—hold space. Yes—stay present if it feels safe. Yes—ask gentle questions and reflect back what you're seeing. But don't confuse **mediation** with **martyrdom**.

You are not here to rescue people from their pain.
You are not here to correct their worldview.
You are not here to drag anyone into healing they haven't asked for.

And you are not obligated to stay in a conversation that requires you to shrink, justify your existence, or absorb someone else's projections just to keep the peace.

At some point, discernment becomes necessary.

There is a moment when staying engaged stops being compassion and starts becoming self-betrayal. That moment is quiet. Subtle. And if you've learned to override yourself, easy to miss.

But your body usually knows.

Guarding Your Sacred Energy

Your clarity will not always be met with clarity. Sometimes it becomes a mirror others aren't ready to look into. And when that happens, protecting your energy isn't avoidance—it's wisdom.

This doesn't require anger.
It doesn't require self-righteousness.
And it doesn't require explanation.

Sometimes it looks like stepping back.
Sometimes it looks like changing the subject.
Sometimes it looks like ending the conversation without finishing it.

Not every exchange is meant to be resolved in real time.
Not every truth needs to be understood immediately.
And not every relationship can evolve at the same pace.

Your responsibility is not to make your truth palatable.
It's to remain aligned.

Healing Must Be Chosen

Here's the paradox: the more you try to force someone to "wake up," the more they resist. Because healing—real, lasting healing—requires *ownership*. It has to be invited in. You can't push someone into a breakthrough. You can only create the conditions where it becomes possible.

And the most powerful way to do that?

Be yourself.

Fully. Freely. Without apology.

Because your groundedness is an invitation.
Your clarity is a reflection.
Your calm presence is a silent transmission that says, *You can choose this too.*
And sometimes, that's all it takes.

Not a debate. Not a breakdown. Just your beingness. Just your peace. Just your embodiment.

Truth isn't always loud.
But it's always contagious.

Story: "The Dinner Table Shift"

Layla used to go home with a strategy.

Every family gathering, she'd rehearse how to keep the peace—or how to make her point without starting another argument. Her sister would make passive digs. Her father would dominate the conversation. Her mother would disappear into the kitchen to avoid it all.

Layla used to try to manage it. To soften the edges. To slide her truths into jokes or carefully worded questions. But no matter how skillful she became, she always left feeling drained. *Invisible.* Like the most important parts of her weren't welcome at the table.

Then something changed.

She stopped trying to convince them.

Not out of defeat. Out of clarity.

She realized her job wasn't to fix their defensiveness. Her job was to stay rooted in her peace. To be the person she had become, *regardless* of whether they understood her yet.

So this time, she came home without a strategy.
She spoke when it felt true.
She smiled when it felt real.
She didn't flinch when the jabs came.
She didn't shrink when the silence grew.
She didn't explain herself.

She just *was*.

And that dinner, something shifted. Her sister asked her a real question. Her mother sat next to her longer than usual. Even her father paused before interrupting. The room didn't become perfect —but it became *possible*.

Later that night, her sister caught her in the kitchen and said,

"You're different. I don't know what it is, but… I feel it. It's kind of… calming."

Layla smiled. *"I stopped trying to win."*

Her sister didn't say anything, but her eyes softened.
And for the first time in years, Layla left without feeling like she'd abandoned herself.

She didn't change them.
But she changed the atmosphere.
And the atmosphere did the rest.

Their Reaction Isn't Your Responsibility

It's easy to believe that if someone gets triggered by your truth, you've done something wrong. But discomfort doesn't always mean damage. Sometimes, it means a seed has been planted—and growth is uncomfortable.

Your job is not to convince, control, or carry anyone else's transformation.
Your job is to stay in alignment.
To speak from love.
To walk away when needed.
And to trust that your presence alone is doing more than you know.

Because truth doesn't need force to be felt.
It just needs someone willing to live it.

Chapter 7: The Unspoken Agreements (and How to Break Them With Truth)

Every relationship has a set of agreements—spoken or unspoken, conscious or unconscious. Some are helpful. Others are heavy. And the most dangerous ones are the ones we never realize we made.

These are the unspoken rules we inherit, absorb, or silently accept.
Don't bring that up.
Don't challenge that belief.
Don't cry in front of them.
Don't want more than you're given.
Don't rock the boat.

They're not written anywhere. They're woven in glances, reactions, moments where something was felt but never said. Over time, these silent contracts shape the entire relationship—dictating what's "safe" to express, who gets to be heard, and what truths get buried.

And here's the thing: **we teach people how to treat us by what we tolerate in silence.**

The unspoken agreement says, "This is just how things are." But truth says, "Maybe they don't have to be."

When we begin to speak—gently, clearly, consistently—we begin to rewrite the terms. We introduce the possibility that the relationship can evolve, that the container can expand, that we can expand.

Breaking an unspoken agreement doesn't mean burning everything down. It means naming what's been invisible. It means saying:

"I know we've never talked about this before, but I need to."

"I've realized I've been hiding a part of myself, and I don't want to do that anymore."

"I love you, and I want us to be able to go deeper than we have."

These conversations can feel awkward. Even scary. But they are acts of love. Acts of freedom. Acts of sovereignty.

Because when one person in a relationship starts telling the truth, it invites the other person to do the same. And once that door is opened, there's no going back to pretending.

That's when the real relationship begins—not the one built on guessing and appeasing, but the one built on *clarity, trust, and choice.*

Every time you speak what was previously unspoken, you loosen the grip of fear and expand the space where love can live.

Because silence protects comfort,
but truth protects connection.

Story: "The Dinner Table Pause"

For years, Maya never mentioned her discomfort during Sunday dinners with her in-laws. Every time, her husband's father made subtle jabs—about her career, her opinions, her "sensitive" nature. Her husband would change the subject or laugh it off. And Maya would swallow her feelings with her wine.

The unspoken agreement? *Keep the peace. Don't make it weird. Don't upset the family dynamic.*

But one night, in the car after another quiet ride home, she turned to her husband and simply said, *"It really hurts me when you don't say anything. I feel alone when you protect the room but not me."*

He was quiet for a long time. Not defensive—just stunned. He hadn't realized he'd made that agreement too: *Keep Dad calm. Keep dinner easy. Keep my wife silent.*

"You're right," he finally said. *"I've been trying to avoid conflict, but in doing that, I've created distance between us. I don't want that."*

That was the last time Maya sat through a dinner in silence. Not because her father-in-law changed overnight—but because she had. Because her husband had. And the unspoken rule that once defined the room? It didn't hold power anymore.

Story: "I Never Knew You Didn't Want To"

Sam and Rhea had been married for eight years. Every Friday night, they watched a movie together. It had become tradition—an easy, cozy rhythm.

But one night, as Sam hit play, Rhea hesitated.

"Can I tell you something weird?" she asked, half-laughing, half-nervous.
"Of course."

"I don't really like movies. I never have. I just... never said anything because you love them so much. And I didn't want to be difficult."

Sam blinked, stunned. *"You've watched movies with me every week for eight years."*

She nodded. *"I thought it was what couples did. But I'd rather talk. Or paint. Or just sit outside."*

There was a long pause. Then Sam said, *"I wish you'd told me sooner. I didn't fall in love with someone who agrees with everything—I fell in love with you."*

They still spent Fridays together. But now, sometimes it was under the stars. Sometimes over a bottle of wine and a blank canvas. And sometimes, still, a movie—when Rhea chose it.

Because the real tradition wasn't the movie. It was the time. The closeness.
And it turns out, that's even better when it's based on truth.

Naming What Was Never Spoken

Unspoken agreements aren't always malicious. Sometimes, they're survival strategies passed down through generations. Sometimes, they're built from fear, or love, or habit. But no matter how they form, they shape our reality—until we name them.

Speaking the unspoken isn't about confrontation. It's about liberation. It's about giving yourself and the people you love a chance to *choose each other more honestly.*

Because when we put words to what's been quietly weighing on us, we don't just change the relationship—we change what's *possible* inside it.

And that's the miracle of conversation:
It doesn't just clarify. *It creates.*

Chapter 8: The Courage to Be Seen

There's a moment in every real relationship when you hit the edge of performance. You stop trying to be impressive. You stop trying to be agreeable. You stop trying to be who you think they want.

And in that moment, you have a choice:
Retreat into the version of you that feels safer—or reveal who you really are.

That's vulnerability.
Not weakness.
Not overexposure.
But *truth shared with love, even when it makes your voice shake.*

Emotional honesty is the doorway to intimacy. Without it, relationships are surface-level at best. You can spend years beside someone without ever feeling truly known. But the moment you say, *"This is how I really feel,"* something changes. The mask comes off. The space softens. And suddenly, the relationship becomes real.

But here's the catch: emotional honesty doesn't guarantee you'll always be met with the response you want. That's why most people avoid it. They've learned to trade connection for control—trying to predict outcomes instead of showing up in the unknown.

But **love can't bloom where truth is suppressed.**
It grows in the light. And it grows slowly.

So how do you start? You begin small:

"I'm feeling overwhelmed today, and I don't know why."

"That comment stung more than I expected."

"I really want to share something, but I'm scared of how you'll take it."

These aren't declarations—they're invitations. They open the space for closeness, not control. They tell the other person: *I trust you enough to let you see me here.*

And when both people begin doing that—when honesty becomes the norm instead of the exception—intimacy becomes a lived experience, not just a hope.

Because real closeness isn't built on perfection.
It's built on shared truth, spoken gently, day after day.

Story: "The Cupboard Door"

They weren't fighting—not really. But the energy between them had shifted.

A week of short answers, missed cues, and that feeling you get when someone's in the room, but their heart's far away. Nora was cleaning the kitchen when she slammed the cupboard a little harder than necessary. The sound echoed through the house.

Liam looked up from the couch. *"You okay?"*

She didn't answer right away. She kept wiping the counter, trying to swallow the lump in her throat, trying to convince herself she was being dramatic.

But then she stopped.

"I don't feel close to you right now," she said, her back still turned. *"And I hate that I'm scared to say that because I don't want you to feel like I'm blaming you."*

He was quiet. Not cold—just still.

"I've been holding it in all week," she continued, voice shaking now. *"Telling myself it'll pass. But I miss you. Even when you're right here."*

When she turned around, Liam was already walking over. He didn't try to explain, didn't get defensive. He just wrapped his arms around her.

"Thank you for telling me," he said into her hair. *"I didn't realize how far I'd drifted. I'm here now."*

That moment didn't fix everything. But it realigned them. It reminded them what mattered. And it happened not because someone said the perfect thing—but because someone had the courage to *say anything at all.*

Chapter 8.5: Conversation is Medicine

We often think of conversation as something mental. Cognitive. Strategic. A way to share thoughts, solve problems, express ideas. But if you've ever finally spoken a truth you were holding for too long—really *spoken* it, from the belly—you know better.

You know that conversation is not just mental.

Conversation is medicine.

It moves energy. It unlocks pressure. It softens armor. It releases grief. It dissolves shame. It restores circulation to places that went numb. It *heals*.

And when it doesn't happen—when truth is stuck inside us, trapped beneath fear or habit or silence—it doesn't disappear. It stays. It settles. It shapes how we carry ourselves. How we breathe. How we digest. How we sleep. How we connect.

Unspoken truth doesn't vanish.
It *manifests*.

Sometimes as tension in the jaw.
Sometimes as a back that always aches.

Sometimes as chest tightness. As chronic fatigue. As digestive issues. As anxiety that no amount of logic can calm.

Sometimes it becomes illness.
Not because we "caused it" by staying silent—but because the body is where unprocessed emotion goes when it has nowhere else to be.

Truth is not just something to be known.
It's something that wants to be *moved*.
And conversation is how we move it.

When you finally speak something you've been holding—whether to a partner, a friend, a journal, or a therapist—you may notice your body respond in strange ways:

You may cry.
You may shake.
You may sweat or feel heat rise.
You may get goosebumps.
You may feel your breath drop into your belly for the first time in years.

Those are not side effects.
Those are *healing responses*.

They're the body's way of integrating a truth that was once too

overwhelming to process. They're your nervous system rebalancing.
Your chemistry adjusting. Your energetic pathways opening.
They're your body saying, *Thank you. I don't have to carry this alone
anymore.*

Tears, for example, are a chemical expression of emotion.
Emotional tears carry stress hormones and toxins—literal *molecules
of grief* leaving the body.
Goosebumps can arise when a deeply resonant truth is spoken—
when something inside you is finally acknowledged.
Even body odor or shaking may occur during the release of old
fear, anger, or trauma—stored energy that's finally finding its way
out.

This is why the phrase *"Let it out"* exists.
Because the body cannot let go of what the voice refuses to
express.

And this is why safe, honest, spacious conversation is more than
just a communication tool.
It's a healing practice.
A sacred ritual.
A return to harmony.

So if you find yourself afraid to say the thing—know this: your
body is already holding it.
And what you don't speak, your body will keep trying to process in

other ways.

Let your truth be heard—not just for the sake of others, but for your own well-being.
Not every wound needs a diagnosis.
Some just need a voice.

Because conversation isn't just how we connect.
It's how we return to ourselves.

Story: "The Lump in Her Throat"

For three years, Dani had a persistent lump in her throat. Not a physical one—not exactly. Doctors ran tests. Nothing showed up. No infection. No tumor. No explanation. But she felt it every day. Especially at night. Especially when she was alone.

At first, she brushed it off as stress. Then she tried dietary changes. Acupuncture. Meditation apps. She learned to live with it. Until one day, her body gave her a clearer message—an unexpected panic attack in the middle of the grocery store, surrounded by lemons and strangers.

That night, something broke open. She called her sister. The one she hadn't spoken to in two years. The one she'd cut off after their father's funeral without explanation, without closure. Dani didn't even know what she was going to say—she just knew she couldn't hold it anymore.

The call lasted two hours. And for the first time since they were kids, they told the truth. About what hurt. About what was misunderstood. About the things they never had language for until now.

At one point, Dani cried so hard she shook. Her hands trembled. Her teeth chattered. Her shirt stuck to her skin. It felt like her entire body was pouring out something that had been sealed inside her chest for years.

By the end of the call, her sister said, *"I feel like I can breathe again."*

Dani paused. Blinked. Then whispered, *"Me too."*

That night, the lump in her throat was gone.

It never came back.

The Body Knows When You're Not Speaking

We spend so much time trying to fix symptoms—tight chests, sore backs, stomach knots, restless nights—without asking the most important question:

What am I not saying?

The body is an honest messenger. It won't always give you the story, but it will always give you the signal. Discomfort is not betrayal—it's a call. And sometimes, the answer isn't in another treatment, another plan, or another distraction. Sometimes, the answer is in a sentence you've been too afraid to say.

Healing doesn't always come in hospitals. Sometimes, it comes through heart-to-hearts.
Sometimes, it comes through finally telling the truth to someone who matters.
Sometimes, it comes through finally telling the truth to yourself.

So if something in you feels stuck, heavy, silent—ask yourself gently:

What have I been carrying that's asking to be spoken?

Who do I need to be honest with?

What would I say if I wasn't afraid of what might happen next?

And then, as you speak... notice your body. Notice what moves. What loosens. What lets go.
Because some truths aren't meant to be held forever.
They're meant to be *released*.

Chapter 9: Words That Build Worlds

"Your truth has a vibration. When you speak it, the world listens—even if no one says a word."

There is something undeniably powerful about standing in your truth. It's not about being right. It's about being **aligned**—internally consistent. When your words, your tone, and your body language match your core knowing, people feel it.

Truth has a frequency. And when you speak from that place, even if it's uncomfortable or vulnerable or disruptive, it resonates. Not just emotionally. **Energetically**. It moves things.

You know this feeling. You've felt goosebumps rise when someone spoke something real. You've felt your heart soften, your guard lower, your soul perk up—just because someone near you dropped the mask and told the truth.

We are deeply attuned beings. We may not always understand the words someone uses, but we know when they're speaking from a real place. And we know when they aren't.

Speaking your truth isn't always easy. In fact, it's often terrifying. It threatens relationships built on performance. It threatens systems that rely on silence. But what it gives you in return is **self-respect, freedom**, and **authentic connection.**

When you speak truth:

You free yourself from the burden of pretending.

You allow others to do the same.

You create space for realignment—sometimes with others, and always within yourself.

Some truths are explosive. Others are quiet. Some truths feel like a declaration. Others feel like a whisper to your own soul. All of them matter.

Every time you resist speaking your truth, a piece of you contracts. Your body feels it. Your breath shortens. Your energy dims. But every time you honor it—even in small, quiet ways—Something opens.
And life meets you there. Opportunities arise. Relationships shift. Synchronicities increase.

This doesn't mean truth is a weapon. It means truth is a tuning fork—it invites harmony, even when it shakes things first.

If you want to change your life, speak your truth. Even if your voice shakes. Even if your hands tremble.

Because your body knows. Your energy knows. And the world is waiting to meet the real you.

Story: "The Name She Never Claimed"

Ari never liked introducing herself at networking events. She'd show up in a decent outfit, practice her lines in the car, and still shrink the moment someone asked, *"So, what do you do?"*

"I'm... trying to start my own design studio," she'd say, always with a shrug, always with uncertainty.
Sometimes she said, *"I'm a freelancer."*
Sometimes, *"I dabble in graphic design."*

Every time she said it, she felt smaller. And every time, she walked away wondering why she couldn't seem to break through to the next level.

Then one evening, she met a woman who introduced herself like thunder:
"I build bold brands for brave people."

The words hit like a revelation—not because they were flashy, but because they were claimed. No hesitation. No apology. Just truth in motion.

Later, while brushing her teeth that night, Ari stared at herself in the mirror and whispered something she'd never said out loud:

"I run a design studio."

She repeated it. Again. Again. Not to convince anyone else—but to wake something up in herself.

The next day, she updated her website. Changed her bio. Sent emails she'd been putting off for months. It wasn't magic. It wasn't overnight. But from that day on, she started speaking her reality before it was fully formed. And slowly, the world began responding.

She didn't wait to be validated before claiming her voice. She claimed it, and then watched the world catch up.

Chapter 10: Say What You Mean, Mean What You Say

We live in a world full of noise—texts, tweets, captions, comments, conversations. But for all the talking, so few people are *really saying anything*.

We've forgotten the weight of words.
Forgotten that every sentence carries energy.
Forgotten that when you speak without intention, you might still be heard...
...but you won't be felt.

This chapter isn't just about being honest. It's about being **aligned**. Saying what you *mean*, and meaning what you *say*. Because when your words match your energy—when your communication reflects your truth—your voice becomes undeniable.

But when your words and your energy don't match, people feel it— even if they can't name it.
You say "I'm fine" with a cracked voice.
You say "Sure, that's okay" while your body tightens.
You say "I love you" but it's laced with resentment, or fear, or distance.

People may hear your words—but they *respond to your frequency*.

That's why presence matters more than polish. Why tone matters more than grammar. Why alignment creates more clarity than volume ever could.

And alignment doesn't just mean positivity. It means honesty. You can say,

"I don't know what I feel yet, but I want to figure it out."

"This is hard to say, but I want to try."

"This matters to me, even if I'm not saying it perfectly."

That is alignment. That is powerful. Because it's real.

So many problems in relationships, business, leadership, and even self-trust come from one simple issue: **people saying things they don't actually mean—or not saying what they deeply do.**

The work is to tune yourself so your language becomes clear, direct, and embodied. So your words stop being just sound—and start becoming *signal*.

Because when you speak with alignment, your voice carries authority—not from a title, not from a script, but from truth.

And the world listens to truth.

Story: "The Misunderstanding"

Caleb had no idea why Lily had been pulling away.

They still ate dinner together. They still laughed at the same jokes. They still said "I love you" every night. But something felt... off. Like an invisible wall had crept in between them, built from words spoken too quickly and feelings left too quietly.

He asked her one night, *"Is everything okay?"*

"Yeah, I'm fine," she replied.

But the way she said it wasn't fine. Her shoulders tightened. Her eyes didn't meet his. And the silence afterward felt louder than any argument they'd ever had.

For weeks, he kept accepting the words at face value—even though his body felt the truth every time: *she wasn't okay. And neither was he.* But he didn't know how to ask again. He didn't want to push. He didn't want to seem needy or paranoid.

Then one evening, while they were folding laundry, she paused, holding a worn t-shirt in her hands.

"I haven't been fine," she said softly. *"And I'm sorry I kept saying I was. I was afraid if I told you the truth—that I've been feeling disconnected, confused, scared—you'd think it was your fault, or worse, that I wanted to leave."*

He sat down on the edge of the bed, heart thudding.

"I've felt it too," he said. *"But I didn't know how to ask without making it worse."*

They sat together in the quiet, no laundry between them now—just truth.

That night, for the first time in weeks, their conversation didn't just sound good—it *felt* good. Because it was real. Their words stopped protecting them from discomfort and started connecting them through it.

And the unspoken tension that had built for weeks dissolved in a moment—not because they "worked it out," but because they finally said what they actually meant... and meant what they said.

The Frequency of Truth

Words are more than sound. They carry your presence, your clarity, your courage. And when they come from alignment—when what you say *matches* what you feel—people don't just hear you... they *feel* you.

This is what makes conversation a creative act. Not just what's spoken, *but how honestly it's lived through you.* When your energy, intention, and expression line up, your words become anchors in a drifting world.

So speak less to impress.
Speak more to connect.
Speak only what's real—and watch your life rearrange itself around your truth.

So if you want to be heard—truly heard—don't just choose better words.
Choose deeper alignment.

Your words matter. But your energy speaks louder.

You've felt this before—when someone says "I'm fine," but every cell in your body knows they're not. When someone says "I love you," but the words land like a checklist instead of a connection. When someone says "I'm listening," but you can feel the door in their mind is already closed.

That's because **truth has a frequency.**
And when your words don't match your frequency, people may hear you… but they won't *trust* you.

Truth, when spoken from alignment, carries a resonance that cuts through noise. It doesn't need to shout. It doesn't need to prove. It simply **lands**—because it carries the unmistakable quality of *realness.*

We don't always recognize it intellectually, but we feel it in our bodies:

> Goosebumps.

> A breath we didn't know we were holding.

> A sudden stillness in a crowded room.

> The desire to cry... or laugh... or finally speak.

That's the frequency of truth. Not just content. Not just logic. But **embodied alignment**.

And you don't have to be a gifted speaker to transmit it. You just have to be *honest.*

When what you say **matches** what you believe...
When your voice **reflects** your values...
When you speak from your *center*, not your fear...
People can feel it. You feel it.

It's not perfection that creates power—it's presence.
It's the courage to be *integrated* instead of impressive.

This is why some people can speak volumes in one sentence.
And why others talk endlessly without ever saying anything that moves you.

Because resonance isn't about volume.
It's about **alignment**.

So if you want to be heard—really heard—start by tuning your instrument.
Slow down. Feel into what's true. Speak from that place, even if it's messy.
Even if it's imperfect.
Especially then.

Because the world doesn't need more polished voices.

It needs *real* ones.

Chapter 11: Conversations That Shape Culture

Culture isn't built in conference rooms or textbooks. It's built in conversations. In the stories we tell, the jokes we repeat, the things we normalize, the things we never question. Culture is the air we breathe—and conversation is the wind that moves it.

Every time you speak your truth, especially when it contradicts the dominant narrative, you create space for something new. A new norm. A new perspective. A new reality.

Think of the most important social shifts in history—civil rights, women's suffrage, indigenous resistance, environmental movements, food sovereignty. They all began with people talking. Whispering in kitchens. Writing letters. Standing on street corners. Sitting in jail cells. Posting videos. Asking, *"Why is this the way it is?"* and daring to answer out loud.

This is the quiet revolution: **changing culture by changing conversation**.

But it's not just about shouting louder. It's about asking better questions. Listening more carefully. Bringing nuance to polarized spaces. Holding complexity where others choose sides. It's about saying the thing others are afraid to say—but doing it with enough love that people *lean in* instead of shutting down.

You don't need a platform to change culture. You need *presence*.
You don't need followers. You need *integrity*.
Because real influence starts in real rooms, with real people, having real conversations.

When you speak with truth and depth, others feel permission to do the same. That's how new values spread—not by coercion, but by resonance. Not by force, but by example.

So whether you're sitting at a dinner table, in a town hall, on a podcast, or at a farmer's market—know that the words you speak are seeds. They may not take root immediately. But they land. They linger. And when the time is right, they grow.

Because the story of a people is always written in the stories they're *willing to speak*.

Story: "The Town Hall Question"

The folding chairs were packed tight in the old town hall. Farmers. Parents. Shopkeepers. Retirees. A few folks who didn't say much but came to every meeting anyway. They were gathered to discuss new zoning proposals, but underneath the official agenda, something else was brewing—frustration, distrust, disconnection.

For over an hour, people took turns at the mic. Complaints. Accusations. Eye rolls. No one was really listening. Everyone was just waiting for their turn to speak. Until Miriam stood up.

She wasn't the loudest voice. In fact, she rarely spoke at meetings. But tonight, something had shifted in her. Maybe it was the tension in the room. Maybe it was the ache in her chest from seeing neighbors talk at each other instead of *with* each other.

She walked to the mic slowly and said, *"I know this is about zoning. But maybe it's also about trust. Maybe we've forgotten how to talk to each other without assuming the worst."*

The room got still.

"What if instead of asking what we're against," she continued, *"we started by asking what we all love about this place? What we want to preserve? What kind of future we actually agree on?"*

Someone in the back cleared their throat. Someone else nodded.

No decisions were made that night. But the conversation shifted. The temperature dropped. After the meeting, people lingered. Talking. Laughing even. Miriam had asked a better question. One that reminded everyone they were still neighbors. Still human. Still capable of building something together.

Weeks later, a community listening circle formed. A potluck was organized. Voices that had once been drowned out by conflict began to rise. Not because a law changed, but because a conversation had.

And it all began with someone choosing not to fight harder...
...but to speak softer.

Chapter 11.5: Immersed in the Deep End

There's something that happens when you stop skimming the surface and start living in the deep end of conversation.

You begin to change.

Not because someone taught you directly. Not because you memorized a script or mastered a technique. But because you've placed yourself in the **presence of depth**—and depth, by nature, shapes everything around it.

Long-format, meaningful conversation is a kind of climate. And when you spend time in that climate—at home, at work, with friends, family, or even in your own head—your inner weather starts to shift.

You begin to:

Ask better questions.

Use more precise language.

Listen for meaning beneath words.

Pause before reacting.

Express emotions with more nuance.

Navigate tension with more grace.

And even if you're just observing—listening quietly in a room, watching a documentary, riding shotgun while two friends talk through something real—you're still being changed.

You're absorbing new rhythms.
You're learning new emotional range.
You're adding tools to your internal toolkit just by *being there*.

That's why long-format podcasts have exploded in popularity.
It's not because people suddenly have more time—it's because people are **starved** for depth.
For layered thinking. For real dialogue. For nuance. For expansion.
And whether they're aware of it or not, they're getting *recalibrated* just by listening.

Because when you hear people speak truthfully, thoughtfully, and vulnerably, you gain vocabulary—not just in words, but in presence. In pacing. In courage.

You begin to find your own voice by sitting near others who have found *theirs*.

So if you want to grow—surround yourself with better conversations.
Turn the TV down and the dinner table up.
Trade commentary for curiosity.
Choose spaces where truth is invited, not avoided.

And remember:
You don't need to dominate a conversation to be transformed by it.
You just need to *be present* with it.

Because even quiet witnesses are shaped by what they witness.
And when your environment becomes more honest, more nuanced, and more alive—
so do you.

Story: "The Listener in the Corner"

Jace was the kind of person who kept things to himself. Not because he didn't care, but because somewhere along the line, he'd learned that it was safer to stay quiet. He was the oldest of four, raised in a house where emotions were treated like inconveniences. His dad used silence as a weapon. His mom cried behind closed doors. Nobody asked questions. Nobody explained anything. Everyone just carried on.

So Jace did too.

He listened well. He worked hard. He stayed out of the way. And by adulthood, his silence had calcified into a kind of armor—one that even he forgot he was wearing.

When a friend invited him to a weekly community circle—just "casual conversation," they said—he agreed out of politeness. But the first time he sat in that room, surrounded by strangers talking openly about grief and shame and purpose and fear, something inside him tensed.

What are these people doing? he thought. *Why are they saying this stuff out loud?*

He didn't speak that week. Or the next. He sat in the same chair in the corner, arms folded, nodding when it felt appropriate, eyes darting away when they lingered too long. He felt out of place. But also… *drawn in.*

Something in those conversations stirred feelings in him he didn't know how to name. He started remembering things—memories he hadn't thought about in years. Things he wanted to say. Things he didn't even know *he* had needed to hear until someone else said them first.

Week after week, he kept coming back. Still quiet. Still hesitant. But listening with his whole body.

Then one night, a man across the circle shared about his father. About how hard it was growing up with a man who was present physically, but absent emotionally. How it left him second-guessing every feeling he had, afraid to be too much or too little. How it made him believe that staying quiet was the only way to stay safe.

Jace felt something catch in his throat.

He didn't plan to speak. But before he even realized it, his hand was raised. His voice cracked on the first word.

"Yeah… I get that."

The room went still. He kept going—slowly, haltingly, but honestly. He shared a memory about sitting in the car with his dad for hours and saying nothing. About how he used to practice conversations in his head that he never got to have. About how he wasn't even sure who he was without all the silence.

He didn't cry. But his body trembled. He hadn't realized how much weight his voice had been holding back.

When he finished, the room didn't applaud. They didn't fix him. They didn't interrupt. They just witnessed.

And that, somehow, was enough.

Later that night, as he left the building and walked into the cool air, he felt something unfamiliar inside him. Not relief, exactly. Not pride. Just space.

Something had opened.

He'd thought he was just a listener. Just someone who didn't have much to say.

But those conversations had been teaching him all along.
And when the time came, he didn't need a script.
He just needed the space.
And a little bit of truth.

You Don't Have to Speak to Be Changed

You don't need to be the one holding the mic to be transformed by a conversation. Sometimes, it's enough to be in the room. To hear someone say what you've never been able to put into words. To feel your body respond to a truth you didn't know you were holding. To witness someone else's courage, and realize... it's possible for you, too.

Jace didn't plan to speak. He didn't show up looking for a breakthrough. But truth has a way of finding its way into the cracks we didn't know were there.

So if you're not ready to talk yet—if you're still sitting in the corner, listening—know that you're doing something sacred. You're tuning yourself. Expanding yourself. Equipping yourself with the language and presence needed for your moment, when it comes.

And when it does…
You'll be ready.
Not because you rehearsed.
But because you *immersed*.

Chapter 12: The Conversations We Leave Behind

When you're gone, people won't remember everything you did. They won't recall every detail of your resume, every post you made, or every to-do list you crushed. What they will remember... is what you *said*. And how you made them *feel* when you said it.

They'll remember the late-night talks where you listened instead of judging.
The hard truths you shared when it would've been easier to stay quiet.
The way you made them feel seen when no one else did.
The stories you told that made them believe in something again.

These are the conversations that don't end when the words stop. They echo. They pass on. They root themselves in others.

Whether you realize it or not, you're building your legacy in the moments that feel the smallest. Around dinner tables. On front porches. In quiet car rides. Every time you open your mouth, you're either repeating an old script—or writing a new one.

And it's not just about what you say—it's also about what you create space for others to say. Because your willingness to have real conversations *doesn't just liberate you*—it liberates those who come after you.

When you show your children it's okay to cry, they grow up without shame.
When you tell your partner what you truly need, they learn how to listen.
When you speak your values out loud, others remember theirs.
When you dare to say *what no one else in your family ever did*, you stop the cycle—and start a new one.

Conversation is legacy.

And the most powerful part? You don't have to wait for a stage or a perfect moment. You can build your legacy in the next five minutes. With the next person you speak to. With the next truth you choose to voice.

Because long after your actions fade, your words remain.
And someone—somewhere—is building their life around something you once said.

Story: "The Garden Bench"

Eli didn't cry at the funeral. Not in front of anyone, at least. His

84

grandfather had been sick for a while, and everyone said it was "his time." But that didn't make it easier.

A week later, Eli went back to the old house. The family was cleaning things out, sorting boxes, debating who'd take what. Eli slipped out the back door and walked to the garden. It was overgrown now—patches of weeds, soil cracked with neglect. But the bench was still there, tucked under the birch trees. Their spot.

He sat down and closed his eyes, hearing the echo of his grandfather's voice in the back of his mind. Not from the last days in the hospital, but from a summer evening years ago, when they sat here with sun tea in hand and dirt under their nails.

That day, Eli had asked him a question.

"How do you know if you're doing it right? Life, I mean."

His grandfather had smiled, eyes soft but serious.

"You pay attention to what your life feels like after you leave a room," he said. *"If people breathe easier, sit straighter, or feel seen—that's how you know."*

Eli never forgot that. He hadn't always lived it—but it lived in him.

Now, sitting alone on that bench, he realized something. His grandfather's legacy wasn't in the toolshed, or the old truck, or the property deeds. It was in *that moment*. That sentence. That small conversation that had quietly shaped the way Eli showed up for others ever since.

He stood up, brushed the dirt off his jeans, and took a breath that felt heavier... and lighter... all at once.

He didn't need to cry anymore. He just needed to keep *speaking like that mattered.*

What We Carry Forward

Legacy isn't carved in stone—it's carried in conversation.

It lives in the quiet things we say with love.
The honest things we say with courage.
The healing things we say with presence.
And the meaningful silences where we *listen* instead of fill the air.

Every time you choose to speak truthfully, to ask with curiosity, to offer a word of encouragement, or to name what no one else will —you're planting something that outlives you.

Because long after your voice goes quiet...
your words keep speaking.

Raising Voices, Not Just Children
The Conversations That Prevent Generational Silence

Legacy isn't just what you leave behind—it's who you raise while you're still here.

And if there's one place where the power of conversation is most underrated and most transformational, it's with children.

Too often, we treat kids like empty vessels waiting to be filled with knowledge. We talk to them, not *with* them. We correct them more than we connect with them. But the truth is, children are not passive recipients of information—they're active absorbers of culture. And the culture of a family is built, brick by brick, word by word, in everyday conversations.

We don't just teach children how to walk or read or brush their teeth. We teach them how to process disappointment, how to navigate conflict, how to express longing, how to name fear, and how to stand in their own truth.

That doesn't happen in lectures.
It happens in conversations.

It happens when we ask, *"How did that feel?"* instead of *"You're fine."*
It happens when we say, *"I hear you,"* instead of *"Because I said so."*
It happens when we apologize. When we cry in front of them

without shame. When we show them that adults are still growing, still learning, still asking better questions.

A child who is exposed to thoughtful, vulnerable, emotionally literate conversation gains tools they don't even realize they're collecting:

The ability to sit with uncomfortable feelings instead of numbing them.

The language to express frustration without resorting to anger or withdrawal.

The understanding that emotions aren't problems—they're signals.

The awareness that nuance isn't something to fear, but to explore.

And perhaps most importantly:
They learn that *honesty is safe*.

When we have real conversations with kids—about life, death, fear, mistakes, forgiveness, boundaries, belief, joy, and grief—we give them something no curriculum can offer: **an embodied experience of being taken seriously.**

That experience becomes part of them.
It becomes their default setting for future relationships.

It becomes the voice inside them that says, *"I can express myself fully and still be loved."*

That's the opposite of generational trauma.
That's generational *liberation*.

It doesn't mean everything has to be heavy or intense. Playfulness matters. Laughter matters. But even in play, there's space for truth. And when children feel safe to speak their truth early on, they grow into adults who don't lose their voice in the face of love, fear, authority, or pressure.

So when you're parenting—or mentoring, or teaching, or even just present with young people—try this:

Let them ask hard questions without rushing to answer.

Invite their thoughts, even if they contradict yours.

Celebrate their "big" emotions as signs of a healthy internal world, not as problems to manage.

Speak to them with the respect you wish you'd received when you were their age.

And when they say something profound—because they will—don't just smile and move on.

Pause. Reflect it back. Let them feel the weight of their words landing.

Because those are the moments that root. That teach a child, *I matter.*
My voice matters.
My truth matters.

And the world doesn't need more perfectly behaved kids.
It needs more fully expressed ones

Story: "The Question at Bedtime"

Mira was tucking in her 8-year-old son, Luca, after a long day. She was tired. The kind of tired that lives in your bones, where silence feels like survival. But just as she pulled the covers up and kissed his forehead, Luca asked a question that stopped her mid-motion.

"Why don't you cry?"

She froze. Blinked. Tried to laugh it off.

"I do cry," she said, brushing his hair with her fingers.

"But never in front of me," he replied softly. *"Not even when Grandpa died. Or when you said you were scared about money. I cry all the time. But*

you don't. Did someone teach you that?"

It hit her like a wave.

She realized, in that moment, that he wasn't just asking about her tears. He was asking whether emotions were allowed to exist out loud. Whether his mom—the person who gave him permission for everything else—would give him permission to feel.

She sat down at the edge of his bed. Took a breath. And told him the truth.

"I was taught to hide my feelings. I thought being strong meant being quiet. But that's not true. You're right to cry. You're brave to cry. And I want you to know… I'm still learning how to show mine."

She didn't expect to cry then—but she did. Right there in front of him. Not a meltdown. Not a performance. Just tears—gentle and true.

Luca reached out and held her hand.

"It's okay, Mommy," he said. *"I think you're strong when you cry."*

And just like that, something broke open between them. Not in a dramatic, movie-scene way. But in the kind of way that changes a lineage.

That night, she didn't just raise her child.
She raised her own inner child too.
And for the first time in years, both of them went to bed a little more whole.

Chapter 13: Living a Conversational Life

By now, you know that conversation isn't just about words. It's about presence. It's about courage. It's about alignment. It's about listening. It's about love.

But more than that—it's a way of living.

To live a conversational life is to treat every interaction as sacred.
Every silence as an invitation.
Every disagreement as a portal.
Every person as a teacher.
Every truth as something worthy of being spoken—gently, clearly, and in time.

You don't have to master all the techniques. You don't need perfect timing, or perfect language, or perfect emotional intelligence. You just need the *willingness* to show up. To be real. To ask questions. To say "I don't know." To say "I care." To say "Let's figure this out together."

Because when you live this way, conversation stops being an event —and starts becoming your *currency of connection*.

It's how you build relationships.

It's how you deepen love.
It's how you lead.
It's how you heal.
It's how you raise children.
It's how you shift culture.
It's how you listen to your higher self.
It's how you become who you actually are.

And yes, it's how you change your life.

A conversational life isn't about always talking—it's about being *in dialogue* with everything: your body, your intuition, your relationships, your community, the land, the moment. It's about living awake. Living responsive. Living in *tune* with what's trying to be known and spoken through you.

It's about choosing connection over performance.
Truth over comfort.
Curiosity over assumption.
And presence over perfection.

Because in a world full of noise, what people are starving for isn't more information.
It's *real connection.*

And the ones who choose to live in conversation with life?
They don't just find freedom.

They *become* it.

"The Coffee Shop Pause"

Jared didn't usually talk to strangers. Especially not in line at a crowded coffee shop on a rainy Tuesday morning. But something about the woman in front of him—maybe the way she kept looking down at her phone, then glancing away like she was bracing herself—pulled at him.

When they reached the counter, she hesitated. The barista smiled. She didn't smile back.

"I'm sorry," she mumbled. *"I'll just take a tea."*

She moved to the pickup area quickly, head low, hands clenched. Jared ordered his coffee, then walked over and stood nearby, not close enough to intrude—but close enough to be there.

A minute passed. Then he said, *"You doing okay today?"*

She looked startled. Caught off guard. But something in his voice —his *tone*, not his words—was soft. Real. Unscripted.

She swallowed. Then nodded. Then shook her head. *"Honestly? No. I'm not."*

They didn't have a long conversation. There weren't any dramatic tears or life advice exchanged. But they *talked*. For five minutes. About grief. About pressure. About how hard it is to keep going sometimes when no one seems to notice you're struggling.

She left with her tea. He left with his coffee. And neither of them left the same.

Months later, she wrote him a letter. Somehow tracked him down through a mutual friend. She said that conversation was the first time she'd felt like a *human being* in weeks. That it reminded her she still existed. That it helped her make a phone call she'd been putting off. That it mattered.

Jared hadn't done anything remarkable.

He just lived *as if every moment might be one that mattered.*

And it was.

Conclusion: Speak It Into Being

This book began with a simple idea: *All it takes is a conversation.*

Now you've seen what that really means.

It means reclaiming your voice.
It means listening to your higher self.
It means building deeper relationships.
It means healing old wounds.
It means changing your environment, your culture, your legacy—
one word at a time.

But more than anything, it means *choosing to show up.*

Because conversation is a form of action.
It's how we move energy.
It's how we change direction.
It's how we make something real.

A single sentence can start a movement.
A single question can save a relationship.
A single moment of honesty can shift a lifetime of silence.

And here's the most important part: **you don't need to have it all**

figured out.

You don't need perfect words or perfect timing.

You just need to be willing to speak.
To ask.
To listen.
To begin.

And when you do, you'll realize what I've come to believe with everything in me:

Your life is one conversation away from a breakthrough.

Maybe with a friend.
Maybe with a stranger.
Maybe with someone you love.
Maybe with yourself.

So speak.
Ask.
Listen.
Connect.
Tell the truth.

And remember:

All it takes... is a conversation.

A Closing Conversation

If you've read this far, you've already been in conversation with this book.

Not in a dramatic way. Not in a way that asks you to agree with everything or change your life overnight. More like the way a real conversation works—one that stays with you after it's over, quietly resurfacing at unexpected times.

That was always the intention.

Conversation doesn't end when the words stop. Most of the time, that's when it actually begins to do its work. In the pauses afterward. In the moments when something you read shows up in your own life and refuses to be ignored.

You might notice that certain conversations feel different now. Maybe not heavier, but harder to avoid. You may become more aware of what you say automatically, and more aware of what you hold back. That awareness can feel uncomfortable at first, but it isn't something that needs fixing. It's just clarity arriving.

Most of the conversations that matter don't announce themselves. They don't show up as obvious turning points. They arrive quietly —as a thought you keep circling, a feeling that doesn't go away, a truth that's been asking for space longer than you've been willing to give it.

And usually, you already know what it's about.

This book can't tell you who to talk to or exactly what to say. Those answers only make sense inside your own life, shaped by your relationships, your history, and your timing. But it might help you notice where you've been quiet out of habit rather than choice. Or where you've confused peace with keeping things unspoken. Or where you've been waiting for the "right moment" instead of recognizing that clarity often comes after you begin speaking, not before.

You don't have to resolve everything at once. You don't have to confront every person or revisit every past conversation. That kind of pressure usually does more harm than good.

Change tends to start smaller than that.

It often begins with one honest sentence you stop editing in your head.
One pause where you don't rush to soften what you mean.
One moment where you let yourself say the thing you've been circling instead of continuing to talk around it.

Sometimes that conversation is with another person. Sometimes it's internal. Sometimes it's simply admitting something to yourself that you've been carrying without ever naming.

If there's one thing worth sitting with before you close this book, it's this question:

What conversation have you been aware of for a while now, even if you haven't acted on it yet?

Not the one that feels dramatic or urgent. The quieter one. The one that keeps resurfacing when things slow down.

You don't need to rehearse it perfectly. You don't need the right tone, the right timing, or the right outcome. Most meaningful conversations don't begin with certainty. They begin with honesty. And honesty doesn't require performance.

It also doesn't require you to be healed, composed, or finished. Some of the most important conversations happen while things are still unresolved. Waiting until everything feels settled is often just another way of postponing what you already know matters.

If this book has offered anything, I hope it's permission. Permission to slow conversations down instead of forcing them. Permission to speak plainly instead of defensively. Permission to trust that telling the truth doesn't mean you're trying to control how it lands.

You don't need to become someone new to live differently. You don't need to master conversation or say everything perfectly. You just need to be willing to stay present when something real is happening—even if your voice shakes, even if you don't know exactly where the conversation will lead.

From here on out, the conversations that shape your life won't come from these pages. They'll happen in ordinary places. At your kitchen table. In your car on the drive home. In the moments when you almost change the subject but decide not to.

They'll happen when you choose to listen a little longer. When you stop filling silence just to make it comfortable. When you say one more honest sentence than you usually would.

That's where the real work is.
Quiet, human, imperfect.
And that's where it's always been.

Bonus Section: The Conversation Toolkit

Prompts, practices, and questions to bring it all to life

This section isn't for reading—it's for *doing*. The following tools are designed to help you live the ideas in this book. Whether you use them in your journal, around a fire, across a dinner table, or silently within yourself, these are the practices that turn awareness into transformation.

1. Conversation Starters for Real Connection

Use these to deepen trust and spark presence with partners, friends, or community.

> What have you been carrying lately that you haven't said out loud?
>
> When do you feel most like yourself?
>
> What's something you're afraid to want?
>
> What did your family avoid talking about growing up?
>
> What's one truth you've been avoiding, and what would happen if you spoke it?
>
> What do you need more of right now?

If you could speak to your younger self, what would you say?

What do you wish people would ask you more often?

What story are you tired of repeating?

What's a pattern in your life you're ready to break?

2. Journal Prompts for Inner Dialogue
Use these to speak honestly with yourself. These are conversations, too.

What am I not saying that needs to be said?

What do I feel that I'm afraid to admit?

What belief am I still carrying that doesn't serve me anymore?

What would I say if I knew I would be understood?

Where am I shrinking to keep the peace?

What is my body trying to tell me that I've been ignoring?

3. Practices for Living a Conversational Life

Daily rituals to help you speak more truthfully and live more consciously.

→ The 5-Second Check-In

Before responding to someone, take 5 seconds to pause and ask, "What's actually true for me right now?"

→ The Mirror Talk

Once a day, look in the mirror and speak one honest sentence to yourself. Not to affirm, but to connect.

→ The Real Question Ritual

Once a week, ask someone in your life a question that doesn't have a quick answer. Be still enough to really hear the response.

→ The Unspoken One

Think of one thing you've never said to someone important to you. Write it down. Reflect. Will you say it? If not, why?

→ The Tone Test

Match your words with your energy. Speak with the same intention you want to be received with.

4. Body-Based Awareness Practices

Let your body become part of the conversation—it holds more than we think.

→ The Conversation Scan
Before a conversation:

> Where do I feel tension?
>
> What am I afraid might happen?
>
> What am I protecting?
>
> What would feel like relief to express?

→ The Integration Breath
After a meaningful exchange:

> Inhale slowly (4 seconds)
>
> Hold and silently say: *"Let it settle."*
>
> Exhale longer than you inhaled (6–8 seconds)
>
> Repeat 3x to help the body integrate what the mind cannot yet name

5. Energy Protection + Boundaries Work
Not every conversation deserves full access to your nervous system.

→ The Centering Phrase
Before entering a high-stakes moment, whisper to yourself:
"I am not here to fix. I am here to be."

→ The Exit Signal
Use this when a conversation turns ungrounded:
"This feels important, and I'd like to come back to it when we're both ready to receive each other."

→ The Reflection Filter
After a tough conversation, ask:

> Was I heard?

> Did I stay in alignment?

> Is this mine to carry further, or is this where I step back?

6. Legacy + Parenting Prompts
Raise emotionally aware kids by speaking to them, not around them.

> What kind of conversations do I want my children to remember?

> What emotional vocabulary do I wish I had been given?

How do I model disagreement without disrespect?

What can I do to make truth feel safe in my home?

Am I parenting in a way that breaks cycles—or avoids them?

7. Group + Circle Practices
Great for community spaces, friends, families, or retreats.

→ The Silent Start
Begin your next gathering with 2–5 minutes of silence before any talking. Then let the first words spoken be meaningful.

→ One Breath, One Truth
Each person shares one honest sentence with the group—no responses, no discussion. Just witnessing.

→ Pass the Thread
Sit in a circle and pass a small object (stone, stick, etc.). Only the person holding it speaks. Everyone else listens. No interruptions. When it comes back around, close with a shared breath.

Final Prompt: The One You've Been Avoiding
Before you close this book, ask yourself:

What conversation have I been avoiding... and what might become possible if I had it?

Let this be your next courageous step.
Not perfect. Not polished.
Just true.

About the Author

Jerry Ferszt is a community-rooted author, market steward, and food sovereignty advocate living off the land in northern Maine. With a deep commitment to personal freedom, authentic connection, and regenerative living, Jerry has spent years building systems that empower individuals to reclaim their voice—whether in the marketplace, at the dinner table, or within themselves.

His journey has been shaped by open dialogue, hard-won lessons, and an unwavering belief that *conversation is the foundation of meaningful change.* Through hosting sovereign markets, nurturing homestead projects, and now writing his debut book, Jerry invites others into a more conscious, courageous way of living and relating.

When he's not writing or growing food, he's likely deep in thought with his wife Nicole, preparing the soil for a new season, or building yet another vision into reality—always with heart, hands, and honesty.

www.ingramcontent.com/pod-product-compliance
Lightning Source LLC
LaVergne TN
LVHW011335080426
835513LV00006B/368